While I Wasn't Looking

Peter Langston

Copyright © 2017 Peter Langston. All rights reserved.

Peter Langston asserts his right under the *Copyright Act* 1968 to be identified as the author of this work.

All rights reserved. Apart from any fair dealings for the purpose of private study, research, criticism or review, as permitted under the *Copyright Act* 1968, no part of this publication may be reproduced, stored in a retrieval system or transmitted in any form or by any means: electronic, mechanical, photocopy, recording or any other-except for brief quotations in printed reviews-without the prior permission of the publisher.

While I Wasn't Looking (2017) Peter Langston
Published by Six Nines Imagery
Tamworth NSW, Australia.
www.sixninesimagery.com
ISBN: 978-0-646-96791-2

Also by the same author

Six Nines (2009) Kardoorair Press ISBN 978-0-908244-79-9
Head Full of Whispers (2012) Six Nines Imagery ISBN 978-0-646-57539 1
Straightening My Tie (2015) Six Nines Imagery ISBN 978-0-646-932750
Six Nines - 2nd Edition (2015) Six Nines Imagery ISBN 978-0-646-945774

Foreword

I have known Peter Langston for over twenty years as an educator and a colleague principal, as a friend and supporter, a consumer of his poetry and reader of his social commentary. I admire the characteristics of resilience and tenacity that influence the character of Peter Langston.

Peter has intelligently walked the land, making an impact, leaving his imprint, raising a family and building a life. Peter is notable and noticeable, his bright and colourful attire are the announcement of his arrival in a space or place.

We cannot stop English changing and so we do our best to ensure that it does not become compromised along the way. It has been the nature of a living language to evolve. From the days of the monks who copied those medieval texts, inventing shorter forms and new languages conventions and along the way gathering with them the thousands of influences which have enliven the vocabulary.

I believe that Peter, through his poetry, is a person who can evoke consideration and effectively communicate the complexity or simplicity of life. I envy Peter for his ability to so successfully navigate the simplest to most complex conventions of the written word. He is a person who is a confident, creative and entertaining writer and speaker.

Language is as much a part of how you present yourself and how other people react to you, as the way you dress.

I recently read that poetry is a trick of language-legerdemain, in which the writer is both magician and audience. You reach your hand into the hat and surprise yourself with rabbit or memory, with odd verb or slant rhyme or the flashing scarf of an image. This is true for discovering some newness of the emotions, and also true of ideas.

I can recommend Peter's latest book of poetry, *While I Wasn't Looking*, to you all.

Peter has looked through the lens of his world and shared his emotions and experiences and like the wonderful Claude Monet, painted pictures in words, exploring the contrast of life, with the delicate strokes of his imagination.

Peter has reflected on the value of the human life with the poems *Elizabeth and Coxy*, commenting on the way we can judge too quickly or draw rapid conclusions, disregarding and forgetting to value a life lived; explored the ability to come to terms with grief and loss in the poem *Why*; celebrated the beauty of the ironbark in the poem *Ironbark*, exposed the need for care of the environment from the reality of our middle-class existence in *300 ft Below*; and celebrated the realities of the mystery and misery of life with *The August Tree*.

While we aren't looking, life has a way of cruising, circling and doubling back on us. Honesty, truth, integrity; love and empathy equal Wisdom. Peter has beautifully explored this theme. Peter reminds us that there is time and that there isn't a moment to lose.

When you are young your whole life is about fun, when you grow up you can break a bone or a heart. You look before you leap and sometimes there isn't someone there to catch you. In life there is no safety net, live life and have fun!

Ruythe Dufty
School Education Director
North West Region
NSW DET

Contents

Foreword by Ruythe Dufty, School Education Director, DET, Tamworth 1

Of Windmills and Dragons and Thoughts of Dulcinea 5
300ft 6
Elizabeth 7
it's difficult to make friends 10
c'est difficile de se faire des amis 11
Old Friends 12
City Cheese 13
Irrational Numbers 14
Footnotes To One Mistake 16
Safety In Numbers 17
Fridge Words—1 18
Little Hands 19
Calling Papa 20
Has It Been So Long 21
For Coxy 22
Cassandra 24
In Plain Sight 26
Tom 27
Ironbarks 28
Abnegate 30
The Miracles of the Misery Mine Café 32
No Stories To Tell 33
The Local Member 34
Why 36
Notes From the Angels 39
History of the Middle Ages 40
Late 42
Winter 44
Contrast 45
The Left Hander 46
Sundown 47
Drawn Conclusions On The Wall 48
Singing Silence 49
Viva Republic 50

The Pyjama Game	51
The August Tree	52
Mother	53
These Lips (A Song)	54
The Last Laugh	55
Opposites Contract	56
Little Pete's Note	57
Yamba - Hot - January	60
Sundowners and Shadowlands	61
Poet's Notes	62
Bonus Poem - Wisdom	64

Of Windmills and Dragons and Thoughts of Dulcinea

I should be scrubbing sweat from last week's camouflage

but I'm dreaming.

I should be cleaning stories from coffee cups

but I'm dreaming.

I should be mowing neglect from the lawn

but I'm dreaming.

I should be smoothing love creases from the sheets

but I'm dreaming.

I should be paying my dues or at least the bills

but I'm dreaming.

I should be changing opinions or forming my own

but I'm dreaming.

I'm dreaming

with a licence from Baron Bic and

a cheap exercise book.

I'm writing.

300ft

Dirty grey whispers
are brushing wet promises
on the outstretched fingers
of Flagstaff Mountain.
They pass by, between leaves
sharing secrets
and raindrop presents.
Gifts left to grow fat and roll
from stem, to tip,
rest there,
until fully pregnant
they drop to stones
leached of character by
a million summers;
to thirsty soil crushed
under boot, hoof
and the light tread
of Dreamtime flesh pads;
to mature grasses
and vindictive invaders
spiteful with thorns
and adaptation;
all eager to accept such generous gifts
rarely offered.
Unaware,
300 Feet below,
we squeeze and waste
whatever drops remain,
delighted and extravagant,
excess now the expectation.
The mizzle drifts down
and we pine for sunshine.
On Flagstaff Mountain,
the clouds are crying.

Elizabeth

She no longer counted her blessings as if to qualify for more.
How would she use them anyway?
The sun still drew her ready gratitude;
not for the end of night
      or some memory of a joy-filled day
        gathering flowers for her hair
          or sand between her toes,
but just for warmth
comforting the thin skin she accused others of having
long before they died,
escaped
the tyranny of the nurse Nazis; and
ordered living; and
energetic children bored with the rhythm of the place and
queered by the smell and witless conversations of the old.

Lately
the memory of 17,
    first secret touches and
        pleasure eased from well stocked shelves,
    was lingering longer than the face
           which brushed her lips so barely
             that there was more
                   breath than
                        skin.
    Only her golden hair remained,
        amplified by the late afternoon summer sun
           and laying in random disorder across her neck,
        folded in gently
           among her own long black thicket
        on a pillow that had never seen contrast.
But her name was gone:
                just sweet urgent touches
    and some vague notion of spotty boys and dances,
      their hearts broken by inattention to their infatuation.
           One long beach-house summer on the south coast.

She could still hear the gulls calling
    their shrill demands drowning the dross of life and time.
      Ancient waves crashing their insistent retelling of mariner's tales,
        down the lane and

                over the marram grass ...
who was she
        this passing endorsement
           of her right to abandonment,
                this gift bearer of an informed innocence.
What was her name?

She remembered the names of her children;
their numb-skull pups,
bouncing on her bed,
touring her Zimmer frame at breakneck speed and
re-imagining the circuitous ward as Mt Panorama;
spilling others' cups of tea in collisions and
reducing Marjorie,
The Queen of Ward Three,
to collateral damage.
Her stored revenge like a thrifty farmer's wife,
harvested in spite during communal singing.
Oh yes.
She knew the brats names,
their nicknames and
their yelling names.

There was total recall of boyfriends from uni;
      soldiers keeping time and vigil in loud paces
          between the Seine and Notre Dame;
              a torrid week
                   humping two surprised Germans in Edinburgh;
husbands, much life, children, places, things, achievements;
                  The Beatles, Dylan, Joni;
                        Phillip Larkin;
                  Whitely, Whitlam, Wordsworth;
remembered them all
fondly
accurately, but ...
what was her name?
Now
Discipline would soon be needed.
The sun was stretching the tight skin on her arm again.
It's warmth
a comfort
It's angle
a strict minute hand

to herald Taylah
and her tea trolley.
Hospitality green,
her bushy blond hair tucked
and trapped in a green pill-box hat,
but her tongue left unrestrained.
Opinions regurgitated from headlines;
but the old were too polite to object,
or too lost in the comfort of dementia,
or too deaf.
"Hello there Elizabeth.
Here we go. Moo and two.
Still not talking darlin'.
Oh well. Maybe tomorrow. See ya love.
Don't do anything I wouldn't do!"
What?
Travel?
Think?
Create?
Care?
Thankfully, poor advice often comes too late.
On she rattled, flirting with the incontinent,
absorbed in her own din.

Elizabeth took her own smile,
        to that remote hiding place,
                a summer beach-house on the south coast;
and prepared for the grandchildren,
the reproach of her daughter
and death.

What was her name?

it's difficult to make friends

Afterwards

when drops of you dried salty among the dust

I saw you reach for his hand

let fingers touch and

take that first brush of palm

offering trust 1.01

in place of unease

just a few important steps beyond uncertainty

preparing the path to home

Much to learn

much to accept

much to gain from giving

c'est difficile de se faire des amis

Afterwards

when drops of you dried salty *parmi la poussière*

I saw you reach for his hand

laisser les doigts touch and

take that first brush of palm

offrant confiance 1.01

in place of unease

just a few *étapes importantes beyond incertitude*

preparing the path to home

Beaucoup à apprendre

Beaucoup à accepter

Beaucoup à gagner de donner

Old Friends

Two old friends
meet for consensual coffee
having discovered
the deceit of suburbs
who's orbits coincided
but withheld
the Venn-like opportunity.

Guilty of laziness,
neglect excused as busyness,
living Lennon's paradigm,
when chance condemned
in the pie shop,
one Sunday morning,
as both played hooky.

Lifetimes lost
to work
or kids
or other things.
New friends
and death
to old dreams.

Mochas in hand,
ideas passed unrequited
as egos vacuum spaces
in the conversation
where listening lives.
Payments made to lip service,
promises to do this again ...

... which are never kept.

City Cheese

Country Mouse, waking, 6:00am

There's conflict outside my window.
A Noisy Minor competes to be noticed,
happy to choose its flight path
and call a morning song,
while aluminium wings
beat and roar above.
First lighters shuffle past,
encouraging Fido's grandson
and watching for discards.
A constant rush busies Addison Rd
sometimes pausing on our corner
for Tina to doof doof her chained complaint
then blink winks at my bedroom wall.

A blue bus,
disguised in orange camouflage,
takes captives with coffees,
in suits,
from under the our balcony,
even on a Saturday.
Marrickville sleeps on,
unaware of the white noise
this city orchestra plays,
as I listen to its instruments
one
by
one.

Anticipating cheddar,
I found Jersey Blue,
nibbling richly
as City Mice rushed by.

Irrational Numbers

The numbers arrived this morning
Slowly invading casual conversation
which might normally be cheeky
or at least breathless
in that space between waking and shower.
"One egg or two"
"I'm leaving in twenty"
"That was a first"
So subtle,
they blended before
the Sheridan's began to drip dry.

Numbers mocked me from the breakfast screen.
Interest rates, balance of trade, budget forecasts
smiled their way past Koch's lips;
highest maximums and record rainfall
calculated the weather guy,
whilst another Storm won 36-12.
There was 25% off at this store
and 2 for 1 at that.
Call 1800 for the special offer
while the PM plays the numbers game.

The buggers had infested MY space:
usually a study,
today it was an office.
Numbers hid in draws and
danced about on the screen;
corralled by cut and pasted cells
only to escape calculations
in the blink of a fat finger.
Pages of them lay in wait
for me to service their desires
in shuffled piles of files,
ordered, indexed, sorted.
Waiting for my number to come up.

This place was not designed for such.
Trees ripple behind a wall of glass.
Birds squabble at feeders a quip away.
The thoughts of great poets wink
from shelves so close
I could tip TS Eliot into my hand.
My thoughts should be even closer
but instead
lie fogged by an insistence
that I must live by equation.

Dreams,
stories,
vague ideas,
wild things,
are all victims today,
decimated by irrational numbers
into fractions of themselves
wandering about
begging me for warmth
and a chance for expression.

Stupefied,
nullified,
mummified,
I accept praise for creating order,
pose for snaps with the filing cabinet and
pin my newly turned leaf on the door ...
... while
renting office space
in some neglected corner
where formulas never reach,
chaos is passing notes to neurons
who see numbers for what they are
... irrational

Footnotes To One Mistake

Since my hair turned white
and groans replaced spring,
mocha machinations dwell
on opportunities lost,
mistakes made.
Mental tally marks mount,
aided by a milk moustachioed party
of the second part.
If my life were a podcast
temptation may goad me
to press "back 30" -
years, not seconds -
for a sterner argument with God:
please, can I make
just one mistake.

She made one mistake.
Desperate for escape
she said yes.

If only the flaws in our humanity
were more evenly shared.
Those who choose selfishly,
rather than badly,
be more often the ones punished.

Loved and obeyed,
for twenty five years,
according to promise,
according to belief,
till he left,
dirt on his hands
but the worst stains on her,
to die lonely,
emptied,
sucked dry of love
and tossed carelessly away
as if she never mattered.
The guilty go free,
the sinless punished
for that one mistake
we all applauded
among cheers and thrown rice.

How harsh just one mistake seems
when my account is so full
of stupid choices,
of risks
and responsibility I shared
so readily
to partition guilt.

How easy
How easy

Safety In Numbers

Drinking a shaky tea at Maccas
shrouded in bright sunny darkness.
Tears,
escaping their sunglassed camouflage,
track to my chin
and drop,
damning my capitulation
in several t-shirt polka dots.
Hidden in the sea of meal deals,
cherub-faced future obesity obscenity
and free seniors tea,
few notice,
then pretend not to,
as if it were a contagion
and let me get on with it.
Suppressing my need for release
and a stranger's quiet humanity,
I gulp my tea
and retreat
to maintain their safety in numbers
pitted as they were
against one man crying.

Fridge Words - 1

jump - with - possibility

each - tiny - rainbow

a - dream

a - simple - breath

laughter

today

blue - sky - comes

Little Hands

These little hands
with so much to say
and no fear of saying them
through brush
or pencil.

These little hands
which can't be wrong,
turn no wrong corners,
paint no errors
from unchastened imaginations.

These little hands
who hear no why
and craft why not
with permission
and baton-passed hope.

Such hands as ours
now worn to habit
but longing for washing
through memories of first lines
from our little hands.

Calling Papa

I hear you calling
behind closed doors
where your parents fret
and feel each nick
each change to your newness
your perfection.

With each question
you muffle cry
I mull over answers
no longer mine to give
having passed my knowledge
to previous enquiries.

Call and response
in the waiting room,
surviving conversation
"Yes it's hot"
"No, I'm from Tamworth"
"Yes, I'm used to it"

Having been there
and done that
offering no distraction.
Nor Donna or Elton.
The eighties muszac
offering no consolation.

I still hear you calling
a hallway away
from my secondary protection.
My old voice silenced
by good judgment
and bad music.

These early elder days
I had thought to be
about giving.
They're not.
It's about waiting to be asked.
Lessons learned all round.

Has It Been So Long

We were thin and you were pretty
You wore her clothes
I wore beanies
We spun our cocoon
refused to emerge
till with no sense at all
we were hippy married.

Has it been so long?

I know where every moment hides
catalogued in trusted engrams
playing on Mondays
and other bad days
reminders
that even your leftovers
sate my hunger

Has it been so long?

Three adults standing in children's shadows
each with a Skoobie smile and
Shaggy's humour.
I'm waiting for you to get old
to catch up
but in any light
you are still hooped in red, white and blue.

Has it been so long?

We can't make babies anymore
(we set out to, remember)
Our quota meets us for coffee
while we listen like our parents did.
Let's birth more memories
on mellow afternoons
making music into the red wine evening.

Yes, it has been so long.
I remember every breathless second.

For Coxy

When Paul died,
the sun fell across his bench
but finding it empty,
warmed it for a passer by
who might fall
beyond the fringe,
to hide in plain view
far from sight.

When Paul died,
haters competed with
the compassionate
for column space,
arguing the importance
of appearance,
demeanour
and what they might have done.

When Paul died,
the Leader splurged,
donating eight short sentences:
two less than the fingers
of life smeared hands
long since disengaged
from seeking humanity
or a spare cigarette.

When Paul died,
the chance for sweet innocence,
for compassion,
left with him,
for not everyone mocked
or recoiled
when told
to get fucked.

When Paul died,
the adults who inhabit my children
remembered a hot summer,
a hat,
rebuttal
and a lesson
that keeps them giving,
grateful of opportunities.

When Paul died,
one or two cared enough
to tell his story.
More than some
less than most,
whilst passers by
noticed nothing
on Peel St

but an empty bench.

Cassandra

It takes two for tangos:
a consolation written by the guilty,
the liar who left,
driven by boredom
fear of age's reality
and lack of spine.
Floppy philosophies
of middle age
seeking younger flesh,
passages to past glories
to prop them up
on conquest's mantelpiece
as though it matters.

Yet it matters.
Life leaves with the escapee.
At ground zero
the refugees sort the wreckage
looking for shards
among remnants of promises
and truths spoken
pledged
to friends and
fathers and mothers and
the mothers
of their children,
as though truths were endless
and true

and important.

What to say,
what to think
into this desolation
where reality might tear
at your own flesh,
so close to the bone?
Bewildered
at some low base,
forced by circumstance,
some moment of choice,
to remain a victim
or find some unknown strength and
be better for it.

In Plain Sight

My one seat isolation booth,

imagined walls bulging inward

in a state of pre-collapse

from the weight of seafood & kebab meal deals,

parts of a red rooster buried under chips and

killer gluten treats that delighted the baker.

Yet walls hold steadfast despite compromised integrity.

Once from and of the masses,

my difference rises above me,

a smoke signal the local cowtends have begun to notice.

As if the shirt was not enough,

there among the pink donuts and plastic cutlery,

sits a man writing poetry.

Sedition has reached the suburbs.

Tom

Australian masters
mastered
partnered in cuisine
with a big Aussie red
in a small plastic cup

I wonder if Tom
would be happy to know
he provides evening snacks
at twenty thousand feet
on plane air

Cheaply wrapped
in card-bored print
pre-packaged morsels
no crinoline picnic
would recognise

We hope
you enjoyed
his plight.

Ironbarks

This I knew as a child:
age wearies us before readiness,
signs too easily ignored through love,
not disrespect.
A broken limb, brown leaves, dry sap,
birds who discover the sky.
A cut here, a trim there,
in order to prolong,
till discontent sounds on the wind
and branches fall without warning
raining wooden insults.
First one, then its lonely mate,
lost their will
to feel the sun for warmth,
the rain for nourishment;
to gossip with the wind.
Hearts silenced,
they fell,
where ropes guided them,
rent and torn,
toes no longer in red clay slippers,
orange sap oozing
from the chainsaw slash

but

This I know, as an adult:
reminded as I am
as branches fall from other ironbarks
and widow-maker's groans
scream warnings
of the crashes to come.
Instead of running to illusion's shelter
others find so convincing,
I adjust my hard hat,
fix my stance
and watch my parents' last days.
Seeing past brown leaves,
broken branches,
shadows on their unwatched faces,
to the days when their backs were strong,
the horizon was clear
and they gossiped with the wind
whilst I played in their shade,
their safety,
their love.

I ready myself,
not for the crash
but to stand strong
in wind and rain,
to shade their dignity
from the harsh sun.
For such tasks,
we are planted.

Abnegate

I've become unwell again
just when we'd all grown accustomed
to my face
shining brightly behind the brave words
of wellness
and recovery;
me, most of all.

'till it vaporised.
Sort of, wasn't there anymore,
replaced,
at least in my mirror,
not even with a frown,
denying me the luxury
of any emotion.

Just a vacancy sign
reflecting back in resignation
and boredom,
as though Munch was taking the piss
or at least screaming
a stereotype
to hide the true, blank horror.

What's the opposite of triumphant?
Whatever it is
it's the adjective for returning to therapy;
it starts tomorrow,
drugs the next day;
and the day after
they'll still be watching closely.

They have a word for everything.
You don't breakdown,
you rebuild.
Your glass,
half full of optimism,
half empty of reality,
is still just half.

The poster boy
ray of hope
shining example of
courage,
persistence,
resilience,
sits cowed in a corner

crying,
thinking about escape
from the smell
and the spiders
and the dark
and longing to be allowed
back to an easier time

an invitation to belong
and the laughter
and respect
and freedom
and certainty
about tomorrow,
beyond the locked door.

It's then
breathing the dark,
drowning in it,
that one long
final
sleep
becomes the simple seduction.

But
I still resist,
scrape at the panels
of my cage,
impose myself on the vacuum
and whisper small screams
for sanity.

The Miracles of the Misery Mine Cafe

The wind is inclined at the Misery Mine
on a dull and grey winter's day,
with chilly abound, to never go 'round
just blast through you, on its cold way.

The sad autumn trees are not looking pleased,
their branches, bone bare and stark.
Just leafy piles, scattered for miles,
as winter draws to its mark.

The rain, bearing ills, between here and the hills,
moves to soft kiss us again.
To sheen the wool cable and glisten on gables,
just drizzle, just mist ... but not rain.

Inside for a time, at the Misery Mine,
refugees crowd the small fire.
They fill up glee and hot scones and tea
and the best pumpkin soup, that's no lie.

When tucker's all done and it's time to move on,
you'll find a surprise waits outside.
For returned is the sun and winter's breath's gone,
and nature is dressed like a bride.

So the lesson is clear, for all who come here,
when winter is a malcontent swine.
On nature's bad day, stay out of her way,
and seek comfort at the Misery Mine.

No Stories To Tell

I've got no stories to tell you
She confidently said to me
I'm just a farm girl from Wiltshire
That's out in the west country.

I'm here on contract for summer
Studying part time to boot
Stopped for a week to visit some friends
As part of the great Aussie Loop.

I wish that my husband would grow a big beard
To look like those light-keeping folk
Just started cricket (and the beers with boys)
Yes I married a great Aussie bloke.

It's funny how life throws up chances
and sometimes we might wonder why
But my kids are so happy and we all love the bush
Exploring our dreams on KI.

I've got no stories to tell you,
She had confidently said to me.
But poets can tell when a soul needs to sing
and I'm so glad she sang it to me.

The Local Member

Let's hear your applause, rise to your feet,
for that local bloke who holds this seat,
who loves to talk and hold the floor
and if the vote goes his way, you'll get even more.
He's a bloke who's not that hard to remember.
Three cheers for our local member!

An uncommon touch and a uncommon man
but common enough mouth, which gets out of hand.
What he believes, is his great sense of humour,
comes across to the press as a verbal tumour.
He's our man in Canberra, in all his splendour.
Three cheers for our local member!

He has a slight tendency to call out and harp
and brag of the herpes he gave to the carp;
or making off jokes about someone's gender,
just because a woman set the PM's agenda;
but he'll still be our man when the others surrender.
Three cheers for our local member!

No one can best him, not even Jack Sparrow.
He threatens stray dogs with graves straight and narrow
Defending Australia, against no matter who
Its hands on his Pistol, calling out Boo.
Well his dad was a vet, if you'll remember.
Three cheers for our local member!

This may all sound quite negative and overly terse
but with a small change of luck, it could even be worse.
What if the PM has an attack of the bourgeois
and takes off to his bank in faraway Panama?
If you think the Mad Monk was our last bad trip,
what if the new PM is the Minister for Sheep Dip?

I'm worried our man might be suffering amnesia,
after hearing his conclusions on Indonesia.
Is it just me or do you wonder how,
he'd relate refugees to an undead cow?
It's Christmas for satirists, or at least late December.
Three cheers for the local member!

I may have confused you, at the end of each verse
My cheering conclusions, were meant to be terse.
It's all in the inflection and often the speed.
Perhaps in my excitement and the pace that I read,
you may have misheard what was said from this inaccurate presenter
Listen carefully ... three *jeers for our local member.*

Why

I wrote you a note
explaining
things
I should have said,
wanted to say,
with spoken words
but waited too long
for the right moment,
for me
as though
I was the important one.
The moment never was,
never will be.
The note says thanks
exposes my guilt
weaknesses
vulnerability,
those familiar things
you accepted
to be my friend.
I just wanted one last chance
but that space is empty.
I'm talking from memory

with the skins of words hollowed and
bouncing off walls
like small, soft, dull gongs.
I would have mentioned your imperfections;
the times I was disappointed;
things I hated;
but I tripped on my own guilt and
stopped at the safety point of
hating you for leaving.
It seemed enough.
So now written,
  it hides in the corner,
    in a creased ball,
      against the skirting board.
Tomorrow you'll still be gone and
I'll try to learn how goodbye feels;
what it means;
because why still swims in anger
at everyone
but you
and knowing why
is fucking beyond me.

Notes From The Angels

He asked for nothing
Got less
Rose high on small expectations.
Took no coins because
he provided no cup.
He could fight,
he could wield a bat but
he could sing
like angels sing.
Other distractions
gifted imperfections
into unworthy hands
to be shuffled and stacked
as houses of cards are
to fall before idiot winds
as houses of cards do.
So many times to battle
only to trudge home,
watch the sunset
dream of days
of undeniable claims
finally approved.
No more
No more
No more
Shout your freedom,
find your sweetest songs
and sing.

History of the Middle Ages

I feel thinner
than
the worried, mirrored betrayal opposite.
So much for silver linings.
I sweat more
but run less
if at all
on knees who scream complaints
I'm too proud to voice.
There's no original left in hairs
whose neighbours are moving out,
scandalised by salt and pepper
then silver
which turned white
in fear of growing
middle aged.

Remember little boy doctors visits?
"ahhhhing" to bright torch light
and thoracic speleology.
They've devolved into nervous moments
bent over a crisp, white sheet.

My skin tears
and bleeds
and bruises
with any unplanned bump.
Red wine delivers
quicker headaches.
Kilos are like golf handicaps reversed:
you put them on faster
than you take them off.

The world has gone to hell
Music is all noise
There's nothing on TV
Gregory Stephen Chappell
will not rise again
ever.

My bowels are irritable
(Even before that crisp, white sheet)
I drip when I zip
Sex marched in sympathy
in the passing out parade
at Camp Menopause.
I was prepared for mechanical failure
but I never thought
a day could pass
without thoughts of curves,
soft blushed skin
and hearing deity screamed for ...
let alone a week.
I couldn't catch a floosy
even if I had the energy
to chase one.

Still all is not lost:
that comes later,
after middle age.
I just wish wisdom
financial security
and a stable relationship
felt like being twenty.

Late

Late
I should be sleeping
or at least laughing
the last pages of this borrowed book.
Instead
distracted by ticking
from a haphazard clock
which shows off every fifteen minutes,
a vortex swims me down
surprisingly willing to be vacuumed
                                                into my father's history.

The every pictures
have stories told for them.
The shelves of elephants
in green, red, clear, porcelain, jewelled
even grey woolled and skirted,
a shrine to Mum's twisted quirks.
Mugs on hooks above the jug
enough to whistle wet the First XV
                                                by a man who lives alone.

A cupboard vomits Tupperware.
Something cheap and electronic and Aldi
beds forlornly on instruction sheets
abandoned to its complexity.
                                                He went to buy oranges.

Quilted rugs
patch-worked in individual squares
by individuals with love-bloodied thanks.
A walker
A walking stick
His picture in the village newsletter
The duty free beer steins
Clocks an hour astray
Four months wrong
8 months right
                                        do the math of little resistance.

Every piece of clutter
a pathway to a story
a mantra to survival.
Where others lost their way
he perseveres

determine to challenge the night
laugh at it in the sunshine.
Stand
fight
Remain

                                        Loneliness, your frequent flyer reward

Late
Tea
I keep doing this
Coming here to be lost
from the future
by my least I can do
Late
almost too late
I realise
I've only been watching sunsets.

                                        I should be watching him at dawn.

Winter 6:00am

A lone magpie
calls once
testing the light
for company
but finds only breezes
hard, cold and brutal
so sits and waits
for sunlight
and sanity
and lazy friends.

Contrast

Eyes like the late sky on a clear, spring day,
cyan burst without exegesis.
Yesterdays of lilies and bridges and white cliffs.
Light caught in sharp edges
of boats and parasols and picnic spreads.
Camille in crinoline and hill-top sunshine;
in shrouded final mask.
Today time wrought new questions
from a tempura of over-exposure,
to precious light;
friend, accomplice, deft foe.
The Seine fell quiet,
the Thames a reducted outline;
even Vienna leaked contrast,
slow bled into pale shapes
and vague silhouette.
A clouded dull palette
dirty with age and memory
paints what is told
at the end of a gloomy brush
still aspiring to light and life.
As flower beds screamed veiled vibrancy
Giverny fell silent with smudged colour.
The rasp of contemplative smoke
taken in paused brushstrokes,
settled to do its worst.

But the terminus
was not the ticket there.
It's those cyan skies
and sharp edges
and light
falling on enthusiastic colours,
observed and told in stories
we listen to yet.

The Left Hander

There's a wet affair calling.
A left hander off the point
all dressed to undress
while a siren song of skin
and sweet sweat,
flower prints and string
sits on shopfront sand sale
to blond hair, white teeth and youth.
The left hander smiles foam sets
and waits,
content to take easy victory
from sex-addled youth
and wait to fight a draw
with the day-job silver tops
who fight for respect
already earned from Poseidon
and the kiss of Amphitrite
in the amber light and
reluctant final white-water seconds.

Sundown

A kookaburra sits in the dim light
passing terminal judgment
on such earnest conversations.
In the age of discernment
we should know better.
Should choose
more judicious escapes
for thoughts than
lazy red wined pathways
littered with threats of intent
and the discards of inaction.
For as the blue turns black
our eyes are hidden
keeping safe our secrets
our souls.
Our mouths bold with lubricant
talk up a past game
only remembered as glories.
The future we worked for
dreamed off
is no more than an endless past
reaffirmed each sunset
with strangers.
A kookaburra laughs
again.

Draw Conclusions On The Wall

My words were clear
meanings not in question
you misunderstood
formed misconceptions?
You didn't hear
You didn't see
You thought of you
And not of me
Tried to trap
But I am free
Of your misdirection.

It wasn't yesterday
silence replaced our laughter
Reckless words turned me away
Your restless guilt came after
You didn't feel
You lost the scent
Your passion pennies
Too easily spent
On other men
And not the rent
In our emotional disaster

Love didn't die
It got distracted
Each day the same
In weeks protracted
The bitter taste
the poisoned menu
Your faithless heart
An empty venue
For words of love
I can no longer send you
Broken, battered, fractured.

Singing Silence

In a quiet nook
singing Riptide
for a safe friendly few
hiding
in other people's songs
their words
your voice
but what are you thinking?
What moves you
when you are still?
Where do run
when you can no longer walk?
What do you sing
when no one listens?
What would you scream
that you would not say?
Why do you laugh
when you need to cry?

How will you know
someone is listening
if you never sing your words?

Viva Republic

It's not the Royals themselves that I've started to hate
Not Dianna's boys or that sweetie Kate
But as a steadfast and dinkie Aussie civilian
I'm not that keen to be ruled by William
Then just as the Royals threaten to stagnate
The youngest pair now duplicate
Over in Blighty, they're a Pommy tradition
But why does God Save The Queen need an Aussie rendition?
However, babies and Royals sell magazines
And special reports on TV screens
Monarchist dimwits still get their jollies
and news of the baby is even mentioned by pollies
Grow up Australia and cut ties real quick
Bring on the revolution, viva republic.

The Pyjama Game

I dreamed last night,
I was playing cricket.
I was a little nervous,
just to the wicket.

The keeper said
"you'll get runs, NOT!
Your bum's too big
and you're full of snot!

Our bowler's fast,
as quick as Starc."
But I just took my centre,
and scratched a mark.

The bowler starred,
she looked real mean
because she played for
the world's best team.

I was a little scared,
as she ran in.
I could hardly think,
amidst the din.

My legs were shaking,
all gone to jelly.
There were giant butterflies
in my belly.

But I calmed myself,
for after all,
all I had to do,
was watch the ball.

She growled a growl
as she swung her arm.
She meant to hurt me,
to do me harm.

I grinned a grin
and set my eye
she might be good
but I'd give it a try.

I'd practised hard
and in MY team,
I was the best
they'd ever seen.

No nasty girl
would take my wicket
I'd smash the ball
and then I'd flick it.

I went right back
almost to the stumps
and waited there,
the ball to crunch.

It whistled down,
just like a missile ...
and left my stumps
all in a pile.

I trudged slowly off
but I was not a failure
because I'd played cricket
for Australia.

The August Tree

The August Tree is pregnant,
their buds gone in winter
replaced by precocious yellow skins
stretching despite the cold
feeding from lower down,
from deeper.
Their scent welcomes me
to take and share.

The August tree is pregnant
with yellow babies
grown through frosts
after promises in April.
They bulge on small branches,
laughing with passing breezes
calling attention to the future
paying homage to the past.

The August tree is pregnant
with new birth,
with earth denied its inspiration.
It's roots have felt the earth,
have held their ground.
A soul unfinished,
denied,
planted them with her name.

Mother

I was there
I held you
Told you I loved you
made promises
for hours
Changed you
Soothed you
until your mum had recovered

These old eyes have seen wonders
beauty beyond even vivid imagination
sunrises
sunsets
and kindness undeserved
and you:
my talk back daughter.

Tonight
Honoured to be among the inner circle,
I watched you sing and dance
and swear and breathe
your own little being,
into being,
by your courage,
your commitment,
your resilience.

Souls
Worn instead of skin,
Hide nothing.
Dancing Ripley into the world
Your beauty splashed all of us,
soul deep.

I burst with love

These Lips (A Song)

These lips have touched soft skin
dressed in red waiting for company
These lips have spoken bold truths
and little white lies
These lips have sipped French wine
tasted blood

<u>Chorus</u>
These lips
these lips of mine
These lips
just passing time
whistling lonely tunes
These lips of mine

These lips have raised party balloons
puffed confidence into your agony
These lips have smiled at friends
spat at my enemies
These lips have whistled my approval
screamed for sympathy

Chorus

<u>Bridge</u>
and they'll do it all again
it's not if, it's when
They'll do it all again

These lips have tasted salty oceans
and stolen gas on dusty roads
These lips have burned in summer
turned to blue in winter snows
These lips can blow you kisses
tremble as they see you go

Chorus
Chorus

The Last Laugh

Until forty, I was immortal
and bullet proof
and full of energy
and sarcasm.
Fuller than most
with my bipolar over allowance.
You still are.
You have to be
or be forever blamed
for abandoning your children
and theirs
and making me your unwanted behest.
Since sixty loomed,
its deficiencies masked
by the dubious benefits
of a senior's card;
we've considered mortality
conceding inevitability.
The catalogue of missing
daunts one into reluctance
and defies the list making
we have deposed by creativity.
Still, there have been weak moments
of mental check boxes.
Dismissing quantity
I am led to hierarchy.
Sex ... tick. Coffee ... tick.
Indignity at public policy ... tick.
But all remain mundane
compared to your laughter.
Laughing with me,
at me,
for me,
because of me.
How will I ever fill the hollow
that remains?
Stoney-faced immortality
was so much easier.

Opposites Attract

I know me mum said she could
when in the end she couldn't.
I know me dad said he would
Till time came and he wouldn't.
I know me bruver said we should
and me sister said we shouldn't ...
but the teacher said she understood.
What shock, she understoodn't!

There's some words just is as is
and then there's some that isn't.
Contractions you think will
until in the end won't.
Where shortening just can not
When apostrophes just can't.
Even though you think you do
for some reason you just don't.

English should be like it was
till Oxford made it wasn't
Contractions oughta be quite easy
but mostly they are easn't
Writing words is jolly hard,
I wish that it was hardn't
Kids like me might be quite smart
Instead of being smartn 't.

Little Pete's Note

It was dark in the house
and each stair was creaking
as down to the lounge room
I was quietly sneaking.

I knew that my parents
would tell me it's naughty
but they always do that
because they are forty

and don't understand
what it's like to be kids
trying to sleep
when you hear a sleigh's skids

up on the roof.
Oh don't be absurd
Peter, you know very well
it's only a bird.

They took me to carols last night:
it was boring.
The only herald we harked
was my Pop's snoring.

They told us some story
Like ministers always do
Which mentioned angels
And with God in there too.

Some kid who was homeless
was born in a manger
and three old blokes dropped in
which was even stranger.

We sang all the songs
But Dad wasn't much chop
Mum all but ignored us
as she fussed over Pop.

It wasn't till the front door
There was a mention of Santa
But that was just a device
To make us kids scamper.

Just before bed
I left out some cake
and water and carrots
for the reindeer to take.

I kissed all goodnight
and noticed Pop's tears.
Mum said "it's 'cause
we lost Nanna this year."

I got into bed
and my brain felt all tight
and I worried for hours
hoping that Pop would be right.

Until the sound of that sleigh
scraping the ceiling
had sent me down downstairs
all breathless and feeling

excited to stand
alone by the tree
and see all the presents
for my sister and me

and watch the lights sparkle
and the candle flame dance
on Auntie Bev's wax Santa
she sent us from France.

The carrots were eaten
They left not a one
The reindeer bucket was empty
Santa's cake was all gone

He left me a note
"Thank you young Pete"
beside Pop's empty glass
and his false teeth.

I don't know what happened
It's hard to remember
but I heard a deep voice
and fell into a slumber.

He spoke to me gently
it was the best dream I've had.
He sounded like Santa
but he smelled like my Dad.

My Mum said she found me
asleep by the tree
with a note in my hand
addressed just to me.

"I put it under your pillow
for you to read in a bit
but jump up beside Pop
and let's hand out the gifts."

My sister got paints
and a board that was rad
Pop gave me a cricket ball
and there was a new bat from Dad.

We all laughed a lot ... then
I snuck upstairs to my bed
to open Santa's note
and see what it said.

You see, I wrote to Santa
a second note, mind.
Told him to scrap the first note
and the wishes of mine.

I penned it last night
when they all were asleep
cause I needed some help
so my Pop wouldn't weep.

I made Santa a deal:
I'd tell no more lies
I'd do all my homework
Not make fun of Uncle Clive.

I'd commit to these things,
I'd be good for a year
if he'd bring back my Nan
and dry my Pop's tears.

I jumped on my bed
and felt for his note
flicked at the folds
to see what he wrote.

But it wasn't from Santa
he'd just been the postman
It was in the neat writing
that belonged to my Nan.

"My dear little Pete,"
it kindly began
"Santa told me your wish
you sweet little man.

I wished I could stay
But my time was up.
I'd lived a good life.
Drank a long cup.

I knew I was going
and I could no longer stop:
so I left you there
to look after Pop.

So when he is sad
jump up on his lap
Say something of love
and sooth the old chap.

I'll love you forever
my dear Little Pete
but I give you the job
to make *your love a treat.*"

I ran down the stairs
and found Pop in his chair.
His head was bowed down
His hands in his hair.

I tap tapped on his shoulder
Ducked my head down for a peek
He wore his sad mouth
A tear on his cheek.

"Heh Pop, it's me
Your little Pete
Would it be okay
If I use your lap for a seat?"

He helped me climb up
Put a hand on my knee.
"Don't be sad today Pop.
You just listen to me.

I know you miss Nan
'cause I do lots too
but I've got a secret
I want to give you.

I'm only little and
I've lots to learn yet
But I'll tell you something
I don't want you to forget.

I'll love you forever
I'll never stop
Remember that always:
Now hug me old Pop."

Yamba - January - Hot

Ice creams as Dad's treat
on a seagull stained bench
while Mum fits seven extra months
into hip tied, crochet memories.
Blow on but still burn your lips chips
sour with vinegar, salt splattered.

Oldies holding hands and shuffling
memories of R&R
on the run from parents in the day,
Vung Tao horror visiting at night.
Nomads and ice creams;
sweet kisses (still) and sunburn.

Teachers on long service leave,
their children still at their day job,
crying sand from their eyes and
catching crazy crawly crabs
in plastic buckets
that would be castles.

Blond hair still tangled and drying,
like balconies over smirks
punctuating surfboard commentary.

Struttin' in your big sister's strapless
with this week's sweaty palmed boy.
Summer loves soon lost.
Bikinis, bare chests, flowered boardies.
Smiles, hands held, crushes, conquests.

Yamba bursts with possibility in January.

Sundowners and Shadowlands

In the longer shadows of the orange hour
they gather to report stories
of the day's best coffee
of the week's best view
of the month's best site
of the trip's best fuel price

They background check through questions
and answers
given in caution
until the second wine soaks
wafers on loosened lips:
communion for yesterday's strangers

Soon an hour is filled with children
grandchildren
familial anecdotes
pride, despair, joy, exasperation
as their generation gasps
at successions unexpected

Bragging rights expended
the asphalt passengers drift to camp kitchens
or small galleys in fifth wheel lounge rooms
leaving the rough riders of longer roads
to their back pages
and idyll heresies

As the dark sneaks in
truth sits down to share
breakdowns, heart attacks, second marriages
till the German accent
jumps from a moving train
and freedom from East Berlin

The writer
dragged away
with questions dangling
in the thick air
sees freedom come again
in a smile in the shadows

Poet's Notes

Of Windmills and Dragons and Dulcinea - my mum used to call me her dreamer. Once I read about him, I became Don Quixote. Sometimes practicalities threaten the windmills.

300ft - written in a Tamworth Cafe, looking up at Flagstaff Mountain on a cold, day in winter. I got to thinking on how we take so much for granted in our comfortable middle class existence.

Elizabeth - one of my favourites in this collection. It's an amalgam of ideas, captured over many years visiting my father's aged care facility. On one visit, I watched an old one, sitting in silence and dressed plainly except for a splash of extreme colour in a scarf, which she wasn't wearing but clasping. I wondered what she was thinking. This is a comment on the way we discount the aged and reduce them to their inabilities in the here and now. I wanted Elizabeth to have somewhere to escape to. The different tabs represent the euphoria which waves through Elizabeth as she remembers.

c'est difficile de se faire des amis - watching a group of actors build rapport and trust, made me think how difficult it is to make friendships when social barriers stand in the way. I've illustrated the barrier by using a different language and preceded the poem with an English only version.

Old Friends - an old school friend I re-met, only it wasn't in the pie shop of our youth but via Facebook. We soon ran out of things to say.

City Cheese - waking up in a flat in Marrickville. Even though I grew up in the city, I can't stand it now. We were right under the flightpath and on a busy road.

Irrational Numbers - I was bugged about having to be doing financial management stuff in my study, instead of writing. A bit of silliness.

Footnotes To One Mistake - a friend, guilty of nothing but choosing unwisely, lost everything, including her life. I have so often chosen selfishly. Seems worse than unfair. I wrote the text on the left and then scribbled footnotes at a later date, upset at the injustice of her death compared to my pondering.

Safety In Numbers - Muswellbrook. On my way home to a breakdown. It 's about stigma and the loneliness of a crowd when you are different.

Fridge Words - 1 - my daughter has random magnetic words on her fridge. I constructed this the day after her first born arrived.

Little Hands - watching children creating without the impediment of age in an art class at my local gallery. The adults encouraged their choices instead of directing them.

Calling Grandpa - my grandson had to have a minor procedure done. This is me, stuck in the waiting room, knowing his parents were with him and reflecting on my new role.

Has It Been So Long? - a love poem and very personal. "you are still hooped in red, white and blue" refers to the top Sue was wearing at my 21st.

For Coxy - Mr Paul Cox lived life on the streets of Tamworth. He was a difficult, often angry man, unkempt and regularly lost in psychosis or alcohol. He tested our humanity in extreme ways and we mostly failed. I sat on his bench to write this; probably picked up a bit of his anger.

Cassandra - a heartbreak poem. Based on several friends who have been left by their husbands. The myth of Cassandra is invoked in the title to illustrate one of them, who told nothing but the truth about her lousy husband but none of her family or friends believed her.

In Plain Sight - writing one day in the food court at Shopping World

Tom - flying on the "short hop kangaroo", I was horrified to be served my snacks in a cardboard box made from a Tom Roberts print and "a big Aussie red" as it was described by the steward, in a dingy plastic cup.

Ironbarks - this is a very old poem and reworked many times before getting to this. The first part of the poem is about two big Ironbarks which once stood in my boyhood backyard, In the second half, they become metaphors for my aging parents.

Abnegate - in March 2016, my mental state crashed after a period of increasing highs.

The Miracles of the Misery Mine Cafe - this should have been in "Straightening My Tie" but was overlooked. This is a true story about a true place.

No Stories To Tell - stories are waiting everywhere. This one is from a NP office on Kangaroo Island and a lady who was convinced her life held no stories worth telling.

The Local Member - there was a day when I wrote angry political poems. Now I just take the piss.

Why - coming to terms with things left unsaid when someone is taken away unexpectedly.

Notes From The Angels - written for Jason Palmer: actor, director, singer, lost tragically early.

Middle Aged - a long complaint about aging, brought on by turning 60.

Late - looking around the room at my Dad's unit and reassessing my relationship with him.

Winter 6:00am - there is something intimate about first light. I often share it with birdies.

Contrast - a story about Claude Monet, which lay dormant for four years as three lines and a series of dot point ideas. I finished it last September after watching photos I took at Giverny.

The Left Hander - one of a series of poems written about the benefits of ageing.

Sundown - sundowners are the drinks had with strangers in caravan parks and around campsites. Conversations are often safer in the dim light.

Draw Conclusion On The Wall - a heartbreak poem, written as lyrics and looking for music. The title is a line from Bob Dylan's "Love Minus Zero/No Limit".

Singing Silence - listening, very uncomfortably, to someone singing and playing in barely disguised apology, using someone else's words but withholding a more important story.

Viva Republic - a bit of fun at the Windsor's expense.

The Pyjama Game - written for kids. A mixed up dream about a game of cricket.

The August Tree - grows in our backyard. It was planted after my daughter lost a child and rarely bore fruit. The season her first outside baby arrived, it was covered in lemons.

Mother - this is the story of my warrior princess daughter who has moved on to motherhood. I wrote this on my phone as she danced and breathed and sang with us, in her flat, during early labour.

These Lips (a song) - a catalogue poem about lips turned into song lyrics

The Last Laugh - this one sneaks up on you. It looks like another "I'm getting old" poem, but its not.

Opposites Contract - a bit of fun mangling the language.

Little Pete's Note - another poem for kids. I wanted to twist the idea of the self-centred nature of kids into wishing in order to give: away from self, to others.

Yamba - January - Hot - another coastal poem, this time Yamba. It still shows my bias against the beach but perhaps softer and more illustrative than "The Beach" (Straightening My Tie).

Sundowners and Shadowlands - an amazing story told to us in a campsite at Minnie Water.

Wisdom - a little thoughtful bonus playing with concepts and what they mean to me.

Wisdom

Honesty
saying what you feel

Truth
saying what you know.

Integrity
knowing the difference between the two.

Love
choosing which to say.

Empathy
choosing when to say it.

www.ingramcontent.com/pod-product-compliance
Lightning Source LLC
Chambersburg PA
CBHW061247040426
42444CB00010B/2280